British Fingerpicking Guitar

Compiled by Stefan Grossman

Online Audio   www.melbay.com/94507BCDEB

AUDIO CONTENTS

1	Forty-Ton Parachute [1:32]	10	St. Fiacre's Revenge [1:32]
2	Lashtal's Room [2:02]	11	Bridge [2:35]
3	Lord Inchiquin/Lord Mayo [4:33]	12	Lady Nothynge's Toye Puffe [4:05]
4	Hardiman the Fiddler [1:45]	13	The Moon Shines Bright [3:56]
5	The Fairies' Hornpipe [1:34]	14	The Hermit [3:21]
6	Black Waterside [3:47]	15	Faro's Rag [2:39]
7	Alice's Wonderland [1:47]	16	Bransle Gay [1:18]
8	Veronica [1:32]	17	The Lamentation of Owen Roe O'Neill [5:03]
9	The Wheel [1:49]		

CONTENTS

INTRODUCTION

I was born and bred in New York City. Looking back, this seems to have been a fortunate event for my musical education, as it gave me many advantages. Rev. Gary Davis lived in the Bronx during the early 1960s, and I spent several years studying with him. Every weekend I would haul my heavy Gibson J-200 and Tandberg tape machine up to his home and absorb hours and hours of his incredible music, stories, and humor.

Greenwich Village played a strong part in my development as a guitarist. Every Sunday at Washington Square Park, musicians from all over the city would gather to pick bluegrass, old-timey, ragtime, pop, or blues music. In a single afternoon, one could be exposed to a wide variety of excellent playing. From the park I made friends with John Sebastian, Steve Katz, David Grisman, Peter Siegel, Josh Rifkin, Maria Mulduar, Dave Van Ronk, Danny Kalb, and others. After some time I put together a jug band with a group of my friends. We called it The Even Dozen Jug Band, and our performing career was short but very sweet. We performed at Carnegie Hall twice, but our college activities and studies cut our stay in the professional world short.

During the first half of the 1960s, my interest revolved completely around black music (blues and ragtime), as well as sounds that my friends were developing. David Laibman introduced complex ragtime arrangements into the folk-guitar world which shook its very foundations. I believe it was in 1965 that he returned from a year at University in Oxford, England. He was just beginning to arrange Scott Joplin rags for the guitar, but in passing he mentioned that while in London he had heard some incredible guitarists. One was named Davey Graham, and Laibman proceeded to play a Charles Mingus composition titled "Better Git It in Your Soul" that Davey had arranged. Also, the playing of Bert Jansch had greatly impressed Dave.

In 1966, my friend Marc Silber traveled to England. He came back with glowing reports of the British folk scene. He had spent some time at a house on Somalia Road in London which housed Bert Jansch, John Renbourn, and a group of traditional English singers called The Young Tradition (Peter Bellamy, Heather Woods, and Royston Woods). I made up my mind that, come the next summer, I would travel to Europe. Marc gave me various addresses, including that of Bert and John.

By June of 1967, I had my bags packed, and I bought a one-way ticket to London. The general idea was to travel East. When I arrived in London, I called Heather Woods, John Renbourn, and Bert Jansch. They took me around to various folk clubs, perhaps the most important being Les Cousin on Greek Street in the Soho district of London. I was amazed at the folk-club scene. In America I had never thought to perform professionally, but in Britain it seemed so natural as well as easy to enter into the club circuit. But more important was the music that I was encountering. Guitar players not only picked their instruments but also sang! What a surprise!

John Renbourn took me to Martin Carthy's house. Bert and John both raved about Davey Graham, and they introduced me to him. At clubs and festivals I met Tom Gilfellon, Alistair Anderson, Nic Jones, Al Stewart, Roy Harper, John Martyn, Gordan

Giltrap, John James, Dave Evans, Ralph McTell, and others. The folk fraternity was very friendly, and before long I was touring with other guitarists. Bert Jansch invited me to tour with him in Scandinavia. In London, Bert and John opened a club at the Horseshoe Pub and asked me to play a regular spot while they were getting together their new group — The Pentangle.

From a guitarist's viewpoint, this trans-Atlantic journey was very important. Many British musicians were still trying to imitate American guitar styles and techniques, but a handful led by Archie Fisher, Martin Carthy, Davey Graham, Bert Jansch, and John Renbourn were trying to establish a clearly British guitar sound. This intrigued and greatly influenced me.

From 1967 to 1987 I made Europe my home. I began Kicking Mule Records from my base in London, England, and Rome, Italy. The albums that I produced for Kicking Mule showed my involvement with the British and European guitar scene. I have taken a lot from it, and I hope I have given it back something in return.

This collection is a tribute and a document to the guitar styles and techniques that have developed in Great Britain over these last years. Davey Graham, Bert Jansch, and John Renbourn represent the founding fathers of this style. This collection presents some of their finest guitar instrumentals.

Davey, Bert, and John realized that an American guitar style played with traditional British music or Celtic melodies was not the answer. It took much experimentation, and finally a new and fascinating guitar approach was developed. Likewise, in composing original instrumentals, a British approach was necessary as well as very possible. This collection gives you some fine examples of this.

I have become very closely involved with the music of the guitarists presented in this book. John Renbourn and I are musical partners. For the last 18 years we have toured around the world playing our solo as well as duet guitar arrangements. Together we have compiled a collection of our duets for Mel Bay Publications. John and I have recorded three duet studio albums, as well as a live double album, all available from Shanachie Records (37 East Clinton Street, Newton, NJ 07860).

I have produced albums by Davey Graham and Bert Jansch. These are listed in the discography of this book. My involvement in these projects was based on my strong love for their music and guitar playing.

I feel very fortunate to have had these experiences in Britain. Over these last years I have seen my own guitar playing change. I can hear a merging of my American influences with those from Europe. This cross-fertilization is very exciting, and it is my hope that this collection will help other guitar players in this direction.

It is not just a question of imitating the arrangements presented in this volume, but rather getting in touch with the musical ideas of these musicians. I strongly recommend you hear their playing. A cassette is available from Mel Bay Publications that presents many of the arrangements in this collection. Davey, Bert, and John have recorded many albums, and from these you can hear their development of sounds evolving away from

American guitar techniques and styles. I have included interviews with each musician so that you can read how they personally describe their guitar playing and learning processes.

I would like to thank Karl Dallas for his interview with Davey Graham, and John Renbourn for our many hours upon hours of talking and playing music. I hope you enjoy this collection as much as I have in putting it together.

Happy picking,

Stefan Grossman

Photo by Jo Ayres

Stefan Grossman and John Renbourn

GUITARS, STRINGS, CAPOS AND THINGS!

Every week I receive letters from guitarists asking what type of guitar I would recommend. Blues and ragtime guitar techniques can be best played on a steel-string guitar. There are literally hundreds of guitars available on the market today in all sizes, shapes, colors, and prices. In order to find the right instrument for your needs, you should consider these factors:

1. How much money can you spend?

2. What type of music do you want to play?

3. What size guitar would be comfortable? Are you too small to play a jumbo or "dreadnought-sized" guitar, or perhaps too big to comfortably play a smaller model?

4. Are you looking for a specific sound quality that only a certain instrument can give? For instance, if you want to duplicate the sound of Blind Boy Fuller or Tampa Red, a resonator National guitar would be the only answer.

A quick look around any reputable music shop will introduce you to a host of brands: Gibson, Martin, Ovation, Ibanez, Yamaha, and Shenendoah are but a few. In addition to these factory-made instruments, there are throughout America excellent guitar makers producing custom-made instruments such as Taylor, Santa Cruz, Schoenberg, and Franklin guitars. It is worthwhile to keep these makers in mind because, in many cases, a custom-built guitar will cost less than a factory-made instrument, will better suit your needs, have finer workmanship, and have a sound far superior to a factory-made instrument.

I always hesitate slightly when recommending a guitar to a student. At best I can only voice my opinions and personal preferences from the experiences I've had playing many types of guitars — both vintage varieties and new factory- and custom-made guitars. My choice for a good "all-around" instrument for playing blues and ragtime styles is a Martin OM (Orchestra Model)-sized steel-string guitar or a jumbo-sized Prairie State guitar.

The OM Martins were made from 1929–1933 (although Martin began to manufacture this model again in 1969), and many luthiers have copied the Martin design for their own custom-made models. The OM has a medium-sized body with an excellent volume, response, and projection. It does not have a deep body, which makes it comfortable to hold, as well as contributes to its unique sound. The OM is a very balanced instrument, which is ideal for most fingerpicking styles.

Prairie State guitars were made from 1915–1940 by the Larsen brothers. They can be found with the names Eupononen, Mauer, and Stahl, as well as Prairie State. Their sizes range from small bodied to large. The jumbo size can be compared to the Gibson J-200, but it is not deep bodied. It has a stronger bass response than the OM and is not as balanced overall. But it allows me to play a much wider variety of sounds — from the rhythmic, smooth, alternating-bass style of Mississippi John Hurt with my bare fingers to the ragged, syncopated, complex style of Rev. Gary Davis with fingerpicks. It is a more "complete" guitar which offers a wider choice of textures and sounds. Prairie States are generally very difficult to locate. They are a rare breed, although recently my wife purchased a beautiful 1915 small-bodied Prairie State at an auction in New Jersey for $10!

These are my two choices. And for years I played a 1930 Martin OM-45 and after that a 1930s rosewood Prairie State. The Prairie State was originally a flat-top, f-holed guitar that Jon Lundberg (a superb guitar repairman in Berkeley, California) converted to a round-hole in 1964. I was working at Jon's shop, and we sold this instrument to Dick Weissman, who lived in Denver, Colorado. The dry and cold Denver weather played havoc on the guitar's top, and in 1967 Dick brought the instrument back to Jon and exchanged it for another guitar. Jon changed the top yet again to a thicker design, and I loved the sound and the looks and became the next owner. I had become disenchanted with my OM-45, as it was dictating the type of music I could play or compose. It was very specific in its likes and dislikes. It was impossible to play heavy, rhythmic styles on the OM-45, while the Prairie State seemed to welcome all types of techniques and styles. After recording, touring, and enjoying this Prairie State, I was struck by the fact that I was not playing an old vintage guitar, but rather a combination of an old body with a new top. In reality this was a finely built "new" guitar.

In the same period, I came into contact with the name and reputation of Franklin Guitars. Here was a maker that was specializing in OM and jumbo-sized instruments. Franklin Guitars (604 Alaskan Way, Seattle, WA 98104) makes some of the finest guitars I have ever played. They sound and play magnificently as soon as they are constructed, and they improve with each day of playing! They are made by Nick Kukich. In 1972 at the Vancouver Folk Festival I met Nick, and we discussed guitar designs. Nick then proceeded to construct a rosewood jumbo-sized guitar for me and an OM-sized guitar for John Renbourn. Both John and I have been playing, performing, and recording with our Franklins ever since. Imagine: a new vintage guitar! The sound has all the depth, resonance, and projection of an old instrument, and plays and handles with ease. Plus Nick manages to keep his prices at a reasonable level. They cost much less than other handmade instruments and, in my opinion, are far superior. I highly recommend Franklin Guitars and have seen dozens of my students delighted with their own Franklins. Drop Nick a note and check out his guitars.

Even though the OM- and jumbo-sized guitars are my preference, there are several guitarists who I greatly admire — Chet Atkins, Guy Van Duser, Davey Graham, and Duck Baker — who all play nylon-string instruments for blues, ragtime, stride, and folk music. *Viva la difference!* And of course there is the ever-popular dreadnought-sized guitar originated in 1929 by Martin Guitars. This is an instrument that I find uncomfortable to hold, plus the sound is far too bass heavy for my tastes. It was initially designed to be used in dance bands by rhythm guitarists using a strumming technique. It failed in this market as f-holed, arch-top guitars such as the Gibson L-5 were much more preferred. But the bass-heavy sound was perfect for white country and bluegrass music, and the D-28 became a standard bearer in this style of music. I do not recommend dreadnought guitars, as the feel and sound are not well adapted to fingerstyle techniques. But as Skip James used to say, "Yet and still." You will find some exciting guitarists playing on dreadnought guitars.

I've been fortunate over the years in my hunt for old vintage acoustic guitars. From 1963–67 I traveled throughout the U.S.A. searching for guitars in pawn shops, music stores, and homes and discovered many an incredible "buy." Today you can try the same road, although the pickings are much slimmer; but you also have stores located from coast to coast that specialize in selling old instruments. Here are several stores that I suggest you keep in touch with, as they have a constant flow of fine acoustic guitars:

Jon Lundberg	Mandolin Brothers
2126 Dwight Way	629 Forest Avenue
Berkeley, CA 94704	Staten Island, NY 10310
Gruhn Guitars	Matty Umanov
410 Broadway	273 Bleeker Street
Nashville, TN 37203	New York, NY 10014

If you do try searching for a vintage instrument, I suggest you try to find one in original condition and not refinished. I prefer a scratchy old guitar than a refinished one. Refinished guitars can lose much of their original tone, volume, and response. Sometimes this sound is lost forever, while in other cases it needs years to redevelop.

Remember, an old pre-war guitar can cost a mint today. I don't believe that a guitar should stay in its case. It *must* and *should* be played. So don't get stuck buying an "investment" that you are afraid to use. This would defeat the whole purpose of finding a fine-sounding instrument.

And most importantly, realize that it is *not* the age, rarity, beauty, or name of a guitar that counts, but rather the player — you the guitarist. You need to play, practice, learn, and love your instrument. Mance Lipscomb used to play incredible sounds and licks on a battered old $50 Harmony guitar. The true and final test depends on your fingers and spirit. A good guitar can only help you to communicate these feelings; it cannot create them.

Strings: I use light-gauge D'Addario bronze strings for all my playing. I find these are ideal for ragtime, folk, blues, and contemporary styles and techniques. They are gauged .012/.016/.024/.032/.042/.053. I have been very impressed by the quality control that D'Addario has maintained during all the years that I have been playing the guitar. You will see lots of other string brand names offered in music shops. They have different packaging as well as prices. Amazingly, many of these are made by the same manufacturer. When I first visited the D'Addario factory, I saw boxes and boxes of other brands neatly stacked. When I asked why these were in the D'Addario factory, the answer was simple: D'Addario produces strings for many other companies.

Fingerpicks: I always recommend that students *do not* use fingerpicks. These are generally used as an "excuse" to play more loudly. Remember, you must play your guitar and not the guitar play you! I *do* use fingerpicks when playing Rev. Davis and bottleneck styles. For Rev. Davis' style, they are fundamental. (But so is the use of *only* your thumb and index finger of your picking hand!) Rev. Davis always used picks. He would joke that they saved his fingers. His techniques revolve around a hard and syncopated sound that fingerpicks help to reinforce. But most other traditional country blues players used only their bare fingers. Mississippi John Hurt's sound can never be approximated using picks. You need to play with your bare skin to achieve his feel and sound. I use a dobro plastic thumbpick and steel National fingerpicks. The Nationals are getting harder and harder to come by. Jim Dunlop (P.O. Box 821, Benicia, CA 94510) has developed gauged fingerpicks that are interesting, although for my taste I still prefer the old-fashioned Nationals.

Capos: I use the Jim Dunlop Advanced-Model Guitar Capo. I find this very reliable and long-lived. He has also designed a more complex model called the Professional-Model Guitar Capo, but I find this design problematic and not able to hold the tension on a long-term basis. I also use the Kyser capo, which is an attractive and very ingenious design.

Publications: A subscription to *Guitar Player* Magazine is very worthwhile. Their interviews and articles are generally excellent and helpful. Their columns span electric to country to jazz to classical guitar techniques. These are written by some of the most knowledgeable guitarists playing today. For a subscription, write G.P.I., 20085 Stevens Creek, Cupertino, CA 95014.

A more folk-oriented magazine and one that I have enjoyed since 1964 is *Sing Out!* This is chock-full of good songs, stories, interviews, and workshop columns. For a subscription, write *Sing Out!*, P.O. Box 1071, Easton, PA 18042.

Taped Guitar Lessons: Finding a good teacher can be very difficult. Learning new instrumentals, styles, open tunings, and techniques can be impossible if you are not in contact with other guitarists. Learning from a book is great, but from another person is even better. But beware of teachers! One thing that I have found in my study of fingerstyle techniques and styles it that there is no ONE way to play. In fact, this is what makes this study so exciting. There are countless approaches and variations. Any teacher who tries to establish "rules" is going very far afield according to my views. Standard music notation is not needed and in many cases can hinder your development in certain fingerstyles. Remember: Rev. Gary Davis, Mississippi John Hurt, Mance Lipscomb, Skip James, Fred McDowell, Son House, and Lightning Hopkins were giant guitar players, yet none used music notation or learned by it. Their music was taught by imitation. The section "Explanation of the Tab System" delves deeper into this "philosophy"!

A good middle ground for learning guitar is via taped guitar lessons. I started doing these in the early 1960s. As I traveled around the U.S.A. and eventually the world, I would give personal lessons to guitarists. They wanted to continue their lessons via correspondence, and this was the seeds of Stefan Grossman's Guitar Workshop. Our catalog expanded greatly when I was living in the hills outside Rome, Italy. I wanted to learn new tunes and ideas. I had many friends who played intriguing arrangements and had fascinating approaches and ideas on their instruments, but they lived far away in other countries. The solution was to get them to tape lessons for me, which I then passed on to other guitar players. From this came lessons by John Renbourn, Larry Coryell, Duck

Baker, Ton Van Bergeyk, Dave Van Ronk, John Fahey, Woody Mann, Fred Sokolow, and Barry Solomon. For a free catalog of the many lessons currently available, write Stefan Grossman's Guitar Workshop, P.O. Box 802, Sparta, NJ 07871.

I've expressed some very personal views in these pages. I hope they are of help in your exploration of playing your guitar better. Discovery is an exciting process, and I'd like to hear from you about your finds!

Stefan Grossman

Photo by Eddie Babbage

Euphonon and Prairie State Guitars

EXPLANATION OF THE TAB SYSTEM

Tablature is a guide and should normally be used in conjunction with the recordings. Tablature is not like music notation; however, the combination of tab and music in an arrangement forms a complete language. Used together and with the original recordings, they give a total picture of the music.

The tab system does not attempt to show rhythms or accents. These can be found in the music or heard on the recordings. Music notation tackles these articulations to a degree, but the overall sensations — the feel and the sound of music — cannot be wholly captured on the written page. In the words of the great Sufi, Hazrat Inayat Khan, "The traditional ancient songs of India composed by great Masters have been handed down from father to son. The way music is taught is different from the Western way. It is not always written, but is taught by imitation. The teacher sings and the pupil imitates and the intricacies and subtleties are learned by imitation."

This is the theme I've tried to interpolate into the tablature. Tablature is the road map and you are the driver. Now to the tab:

Each space indicates a string. The top space represents the first string, the second space the second string, etc. A zero means an open string, a number in a space indicates the fretted position. For instance, a "1" in a space indicates the 1st fret of that string.

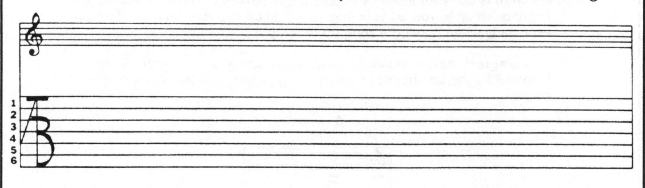

In the diagram below, the zero is on the second string and indicates that the open second string is played. The "1" is placed on the third string's space and signifies the 1st fret of the third string. Likewise, the "4" is in the fourth space and indicates the 4th fret of the fourth string:

Generally, for fingerpicking styles, you will be playing with the thumb, index, and middle fingers of your picking hand. To indicate the picking finger in tab, the stems go up and down from the numbers:

1. A stem means that your thumb strikes the note.

2. If a stem is up, your index or middle finger strikes the note. The choice of finger is left up to you, as your fingers will dictate what is most comfortable, especially when playing a song up to tempo!

3. The diagram below shows an open sixth string played with the thumb followed by the 2nd fret of the third string played with the index or middle finger:

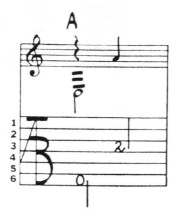

In most cases the thumb will play an alternating bass pattern, usually on the bass strings. The index and middle fingers play melodic notes on the first, second, and third strings. Please remember this is not a rule; there are many exceptions.

In fingerpicking, there are two "picking" styles: regular picking and "pinching" two notes together. A pinch is shown in the tab by a line connecting two notes. A variation of this can also be two treble notes pinched with a bass note. Follow the example below from left to right:

1. The open sixth string is played with the thumb.

2. The 1st fret of the sixth string is pinched together with the 3rd fret of the third string. The sixth string is played with the thumb, the third string with the index finger.

3. The thumb strikes the 3rd fret of the fourth string.

4. The 1st fret/sixth string is played with the thumb; it's pinched with two notes in the treble. The index and middle fingers strike the 1st fret/first string and the 3rd fret/second string.

5. The next note is the index finger hitting the 1st fret/second string.

6. Lastly, the bass note is played with the thumb on the 3rd fret/fourth string.

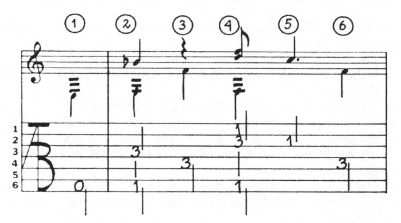

There are certain places in blues and contemporary guitar that call for the use of either strumming techniques or accented bass notes. The tab illustrates these as follows:

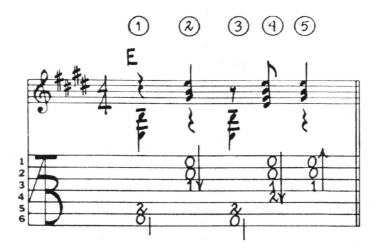

1. The thumb hits the open sixth string, and the 2nd fret on the first string should also sound. For example, play an E chord. Now strike the open sixth string and vary the force of your attack. Try hitting it hard enough so that the fifth string vibrates, as well. This technique is very important for developing a full sound and the right alternating bass sound.

2. Next, the arrow notation indicates a brush, and the arrowhead indicates the direction of the brush.

   a. If the arrowhead is pointed down, the hand brushes up toward the sixth string.
   b. If pointed up, the hand brushes down toward the first string.
   c. The number of strings to be played by the brush is shown by the length of the arrow. For example, this arrow shows a brush up toward the sixth string, but indicates to strike only the first, second, and third strings.
   d. The brush can be done with your whole hand, index finger, or middle and ring fingers. Let comfort plus a full and "right" sound guide your choice.

3. The third set of notes again shows the sixth string/open bass note played with the thumb and being struck hard enough to make the fifth string/second fretted position sound.

4. Once more, an arrow pointed downward indicates a brush up. This example forms an E chord, and the brush up includes the first, second, third, and fourth strings.

5. The last set of notes has an arrow pointed upward, indicating a brush downward striking the first, second, and third strings.

Here are several effects that are also symbolized in tablature:

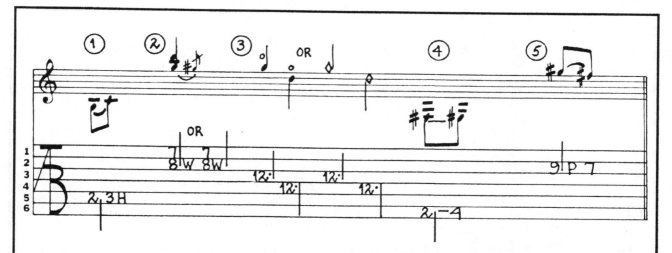

1. **Hammer-On:** Designated by an "H" which is placed after the stem on the fret to be hammered. In the example above, fret the 2nd fret/fifth string and pick it with your thumb. Then "hammer-on" (hit hard) the 3rd fret/fifth string, i.e. fret the 3rd fret/fifth string. This is an all-in-one, continuous motion which will produce two notes rapidly with one picking-finger strike.

2. **Wham:** Designated by a "W." In the example the 8th fret/second string is "whammed" and played with the 7th fret/first string. Both notes are played together with your index and middle fingers respectively. The whammed note is "stretched." We do this by literally bending the note up. We can wham the note up a half tone, full tone, etc.

3. **Harmonics:** Symbolized by a dot (•). To play a harmonic, gently lay your finger directly above the indicated fret. (Don't press down!) The two notes in the example are both harmonics. The first on the 12th fret/third string is played with the index/middle finger, while the second — 12th fret/fourth string — is played with the thumb.

4. **Slide:** Shown with a dash (—). Play the 2nd fret/sixth string and then slide up to the 4th fret of the sixth string. This is a continuous movement; the string is struck once with your thumb.

5. **Pull-Off:** Designated with a "P." Fret both the 7th and 9th frets on the second string. Play the 9th fret with your index/middle finger and then quickly remove it in the same stroke, leaving the 7th fret/second string. Pull-offs are generally in a downward direction.

6. In certain cases, other specific symbols are added to the tab. For instance:

    a. **Artificial Harmonics:** An "X" is placed after the fretted position.
    b. **Snapping:** For snapping a note, an indication may be given with a symbol or the written word.

Many times these special techniques are combined; for instance, putting a pull-off and a hammer-on together. Coordination of your fretting and picking hands will be complex initially, but the end results are exciting and fun to play.

Davey Graham

DAVEY GRAHAM

A. Before, your conversation was, "Do you like avant garde? Do you like funk and jazz?," for example. Now there seems to be no area which has retained its identity. Everything seems to be a vast miasma of music. There doesn't seem to be any level or category anymore. I feel quite lost in some ways.

Q. Haven't you played a part in that?

A. Yes, by evading definition, which I hold to be important because I disagree with Noel Coward on something. He said, "The function of the artist is to entertain and to amuse." I felt more that it was to educate, as well. At least I did.

Q. Coward educated in many ways.

A. Yes, certainly. But when he was asked to define entertainment...at variance with my own approach. Still it's just a difference of kind, isn't it?

Q. You've had a break from the music. You took a day job. Your first?

A. Yes it was.

Q. Why did you do that?

A. It was just to fill in the time. I felt that I would get some more work this winter. I didn't want to be completely wasting time through the summers. So I did that for a month, heaving great big TV sets about. I thought I might take up piano tuning, which is a two-year course. Then found that the place where I would have to go every morning was miles away from where I lived. So I abandoned that idea. Then, also, various members of my family encouraged me to go on playing. I think it's obvious to any solo musician that he's got to fill in his time because he's going to be alone a great deal of the time. When I'm at home, other people have gone to work, you know. Still, the benefits are that you lead the sort of life you want to, in a sense. You don't have to be up and out at 9 o'clock in the morning. Usually, if you've got a heavy concert, you can always drive 24 hours beforehand, which is what I've been doing.

Q. Why did you consider giving up music?

A. I felt tired. I felt all played out, you know. The other thing was that before I had signed with Kicking Mule Record Company I felt that, if I had anything more to say, I'd better say it rather quickly because otherwise I would vanish completely. I was out of work for about a year, to tell you the truth. I took a back seat rather, apart from a couple of gigs at the Half Moon in Putney. I hadn't been playing around very much.

Q. And yet, you're now playing better than I've heard you play for a long time, I think.

A. Well, I'm playing as well as ever. I've changed over to nylon strings to improve my technique. And it has, to some extent, improved my technique. I have to practice a number of classical pieces every day now, whereas with jazz you don't *have* to practice necessarily. I want to make the guitar a complete voice. I think it's orchestral possibilities on the classical guitar that John Williams and Segovia have done so well. I think that it's important to give it a — how shall I put this — yes, a complete voice. So that it doesn't *need* anything else. I'm not really against working with other musicians; I like joining other musicians. If you know they can play jazz standards and they play according to chord symbols, then that's quite simple. If you meet someone who plays clawhammer, you can't just sit down and jam. It's not really very interesting. I was hoping to do some duets with John Renbourn, but he lives such an enormous way away. Mind you, he managed to do them with Stefan. I'm still very much into listening to John McLaughlan, you know, *Shackti,* a wonderful record. Joe Pass, who I love. I also love Jim Hall's work.

Interviews, previous interviews failed to get across something I *should* have really said, which was that my early playing owed quite a lot to Brownie McGhee in particular and to Snooks Eaglin, just as much to Lonnie Johnson. That was something that I really wanted to say that I'd forgotten.

Q. Why did you take up another instrument?

A. I don't know. It's absurd, really, because I don't drive and it's hard to get instruments around. It's just that I'm after a more authentic sound. Since I stopped playing Indian-type things on the guitar, I tried to learn them on the appropriate instrument. I found, for example, that if you play the guitar the sitar isn't for you at all because it wears a very deep cut in your index finger.

Q. The sitar does?

A. Yes, it's like a cheese wire, too, when you slide your finger up.... It's quite a hard action. Although I'm still interested in the theory in a general way. I love the music of Turkey, the flute music of Turkey on the ney, that lovely flute they have — open-ended flute. I haven't done anything Oriental, as such, for quite a long time now. I'm mainly concentrating on the pipe tunes. Apart from the Chieftains, my main thing that has really turned me on has been the John McLaughlan acoustic group. I think that's really wonderful. He's a completely realized guitar player.

I don't know to what extent I'm a folk hero any more. Most of the people who get to hear me now at the universities are ruling the world now. Whereas ten years ago — which doesn't seem a long time ago — they all knew who I was. For example, when I went to Toulouse, the guys who were organizing had pictures of John Renbourn all over the place, all his records and stuff. So it just goes to show you how the hero changes. I just want to be appreciated for variety. I think variety is what my playing offers people.

Q. Are the problems of playing the oud and the sirod different from playing the guitar?

A. Yes they are — different hand positions. An oud, much like a mandolin in shape, is quite difficult to keep still while you're playing. It's a prerequisite of lute playing of any kind — you've really got to sit practicing motionless while you do play. The sirod, yes, because it's played with the fingernail on the index finger of the first hand. And again, on Indian instruments, you only use two fingers on the left hand to play them. No, my main problem with playing so many instruments now is getting them about. That's the main problem.

Q. Is there anything from the playing of the oud and the sirod which has fed back into your guitar playing?

A. No, because it's a melodic system; it's not a harmonic system. With the exception of the Irish pipe tunes, which are also a melodic system with the occasional bit of Italian influence — you know, Renaissance effect. They're all melodic, with the penchant for the minor key, which isn't always characteristic of European classical music or Renaissance music. I don't think there's any feedback, really. It's become rather a separate thing. If I'm doing a residency, I take one of them along as a novelty instead of playing the pipe tunes. What I need, I'm afraid, is a chauffeur at the door!

I don't know how independent I am these days. I don't have quite enough energy for all-night parties, either. After the gig I just want my bed, a nice hotel room, or perhaps my companion, whoever travels with me, a cup of peppermint tea, a radio, and a smoke. I don't really feel like an all-night party after a gig, you know. I wish more people would be considerate toward musicians about that. Another thing is playing over vast distances. Duck Baker told me he was completely wiped out when he arrived in Australia to do a tour there. I'd love to travel. One likes to be at a gig early. One likes to be able to run over the PA system and make sure that the people aren't going to be let in after you've started playing. Also, there's not a bar at the end of the room.

Q. You don't have a manager or an agent now?

A. No, I don't know. I have someone who helps me with my flat and things like that which I never could handle particularly well. Mind you, I'm beginning to feel my age a little bit.

Q. How old are you?

A. I'm 36...beginning to feel it. When I think of Segovia and these marvelous people like Vladimir Horovitz, more particularly conductors, how long they all seem to live. Have you noticed that? All the conductors seem to live a long time, don't they? Longevity runs in my family on both sides. I know what Steve Benbow meant when he said that he felt nauseous before gigs. Because, as you know, he became a taxi driver. I know what that's like. It's like butterflies, but they're at the wrong time of the day. You think, "Oh dear, I'd better eat something." A terrible weightless feeling in the midriff, you know. Yeah, I think my only personal problem is that I have too much time to myself, too much time to become unsure of myself.

Q. I would have said you were a very contained person, that you had your head together.

A. Yes, I am. I mean, I'm not amused by drug parties and things like that. I think they're all a waste of time. I have integrity, which is all right. I haven't got any complaints to make, really. Except that usual ones like, as I mentioned before, bars in the same room as you're going to play in.

Q. When you first started, you were playing in Nick's Diner, weren't you?

A. That's right. That was quite noisy, but that was more like practicing to an audience because they weren't listening to me specifically. I was background music, and I didn't mind it then. I think standards of playing have probably remained the same, though. I think people do too much talking on stage. I don't know whether I mean concerts or whether I mean clubs when I say this, but I think if you're there to play, play. If you can tell a good joke, tell a good joke. I'm against what I think everybody would agree with me about is piss-artists. I'm really against them. I don't think they should have the reputation that they have just because they turn up to all their gigs. I don't think that's where it's at. I always aim at a professional standard of playing. That's what I aim for. Since I've been playing the classic guitar, the practicing has got a little harder, although my style is improving. Still improving, I think.

Q. Let's talk about when you started playing guitar.

A. My very first gig was in the Troubadour. When I actually started, we all used to go to the Gyre and Gimble in John Adams Street near Charing Cross. This is going back to about '56, and then there were several night spots where one could play until the small hours — the Nucleus, the Farm, the Blue Room — next to was the year...in fact, those times were when I met Josh White, Sister Houston, and Jack Elliot.

Q. How long have you been playing guitar?

A. I started when I was 16, in '56. I'd just been to see a concert with Lionel Hampton and Humphrey Lyttleton and Trevor Havelson. It was when Trevor Havelson had just come back from South Africa, and they were trying to raise some money for hostages there. That was my first jazz concert. Yes, Lionel Hampton really impressed me — marvellous. It took over the homework; it took over the studying, really.

Q. Were you a good student at school?

A. Very average, indeed. The only things I were good at were gymnastics and languages. Recently, I've been taking a sort of refresher course in arithmetic because it's always been a rather poor subject with me.

Q. I would have thought that you were quite good at mathematics.

A. No, unfortunately I seem to give a good impression all the time, but I'm not really as gifted as all that.

Q. I have this image of you as having a rather precise, even pedantic, mind.

A. Yes, I have, actually. I don't think I'm half as interesting as I'm made out to be, really.

Q. You must have lived in London for many, many years.

A. I have lived in London most of the time, largely because my mother lives in London. I don' know what the other reasons are. Lately I've begun to wonder whether I'm the traveling-man type or not because taking planes everywhere is not as much fun, as I'm sure you realize. I did judo for a few years. I had to give it up, though, because with the classic style you need fairly long nails, and you need very short ones for judo, otherwise they break and bend. So three or four years ago when I was living in Kent, I did a sort of a refresher course on judo, and I did a bit of weight lifting when I came back to London. I had to knock it off, though, because it doesn't agree with guitar playing.

Q. Do you keep very fit?

A. Reasonably fit. Lately I haven't been doing much in the way of exercise.

Q. The Hampton concert inspired you to play the guitar?

A. No, I had already started. I'd heard Big Bill Broonzy. I'd heard Josh White, and I'd heard Brownie McGhee.

Q. Who was the first guitarist you heard?

A. Oh, the first guitarist I heard was Vincente Gomez, who John Pass quotes quite often as being an early influence.

Q. What benefits have you gotten from playing steel-string guitar for playing nylon-string guitar?

A. None, because they're so completely different. The tendency of nylon strings is to run away from underneath the finger unless the point of contact is completely perpendicular over it. Since a lot of jazz and folk players play with the guitar on their right knee instead of their left knee, this means a completely different approach to fingering. I tried playing standing for quite a long time. For a couple of years, I used to do all my gigs standing with a strap. I have found that sitting is the most comfortable position to play in. It's not by any means easy to play the classic guitar. I think it's very demanding. As you know, lots of jazz players discount it outright because it's not comfortable, it doesn't give quick results — which it certainly doesn't.

Q. Since it's more demanding, does it improve your steel-string playing?

A. I don't know, because I play less steel-string than I used to, generally speaking. I use a different tuning. I use a pipe tuning for playing the Irish pieces. The second…the B string is tuned down in turn to A; and the third, the G string, is tuned down a tone and a half to E. So you get E-A-D-E-A-E. Martin Carthy taught me the tuning. All I've been using is D tuning for quite a long time. I found that it was limited. It would only play Oriental, perhaps Indian scales, but it wouldn't play Irish pipe tunes. You do need a special tuning to play the pipe tunes.

Q. Do you feel happy with the way your career is going now?

A. Well, it's picking up again. I need a lot of encouragement, although it's not widely realized, but I need as much encouragement as anybody else. I perhaps give the impression that I'm very self-sufficient.

Q. So you got discouraged when you weren't getting too much work?

A. Yes, I did. I almost reached the point where I thought I couldn't do it, which you do if you're out of work for any length of time, which is why I took up the temporary job. I still do quite a lot of reading. I'm still Orientally inclined mentally speaking, something of a mystic, a bit of a recluse. Apart from the occasional party and seeing people on Saturdays, I spend a great deal of time alone, probably too much.

Q. Is it a choice, or is it forced upon you? Earlier you were talking about being lonely. Now you're talking about being a recluse.

A. Well I've just seen that film on Howard Hughes. I'd hate to wind up like that. I think inherited wealth is as much of a curse as it is a blessing because — whichever way you look at it — you need a personal regiment of discipline whatever you do and whoever you are. I just try to keep reasonably fit. I feel quite surprised about everything, actually. I don't really know what to say. I'm hoping the work will keep coming in. I'd like to make good records, just keep up the standards that I've made or that other people are making.

Q. What's your opinion of your recorded work over the years? Are you pleased with it?

A. Generally speaking, I think it's what you might expect…. I'm going to say what you would expect me to say — I think it's improved gradually. My singing is much better than it used to be. People ask me to sing much more often, they like me singing the blues very much. I think steadily it has improved.

Q. Do any of your recordings embarrass you?

A. One or two of them do. I missed out a verse here and there on a couple of traditional songs, which I would much rather not have done.

Q. I was thinking technically.

A. Technically I've improved, there's no doubt about it. Yes, they do embarrass me. When I was influenced by the Indian playing, the playing of Ravi Shanker and the playing of Ali Akbaskhe, I wasn't really sure that I was playing the right scales until I went into it some years later in more detail.

I think playing gets harder as you go on because you are satisfied with less, all the time being professionals. That's why you've got to have a hobby, so you've not got your mind too much on the job. At the moment my hobby is just reading.

Q. You described yourself as a mystic and that your ideas had been influenced by Sufism. Is that still so?

A. Yes, I think so — the completely zany character of Nasruddin. I don't know if you've read his stories. He's a folk hero of the Arab world. One of his stories was, he sees the ocean for the first time in his life. He dips his finger into the water and tastes it. He says, "To think that something with such pretensions is not even worth drinking." He wrote some marvellous stories.

Q. Do you do more traveling now than you used to?

A. I'm beginning to travel again. I like every gig arranged down to the last detail. You know, the fact there'll be two microphones, a footstool, that I'll have a comfortable chair. Also, that my needs as an individual are met. I don't like parties after the gig and all that. There's not much you can do on tour. I like to have a companion with me on my gigs.

Q. What type of gigs are you doing?

A. Universities, one or two folk clubs.

Q. Do you prefer that?

A. I don't really know which I like more. They both make me nervous if there's any hitch at all in the organization. I like to be very highly organized.

Q. It's more difficult to be organized in a folk-club situation.

A. Than it's going to be in a university, yes.

Q. Very few folk clubs will have a footstool.

A. Yes, why are they like that? It's only got to be at a certain height, otherwise you've got that thing where you're resting on your toe and your leg is shaking, the adrenaline sort of thing, so you've got to be a little higher than that because it's more comfortable.

Q. You still give lessons?

A.   I don't at the moment. From time to time I do. When I was a folk hero, I was having lots of attention from people. Now there seems to be lots of people in the same position. I don't know to what extent I've influenced the latest crop of guitar players. I don't know if I have at all, apart from one recording success, one or two. I mean, they don't seem to have heard a lot of my work. My own listening taste is very wide, from Hindu chanting of the Veedas to the Irish pipe tunes and even Karanchie's poetry chants.

Q.   Jazz?

A.   Jazz, yes of course. I always did like a blues-oriented jazz, funky style of Horace Silvers. What I particularly *don't* like is free-form a la Schoenberg-type of music. I'm not very fond of choirs. I'd much rather hear solo voices.

Q.   Chanting isn't solo voices.

A.   Well, they don't sing in harmony, they sing in unison. If you take bop, for example, without a Latin feel, it doesn't have an awful lot to recommend it, really. A lot of Eric Dolphy's things left me wondering what was happening, really. Even Coltrane, some of his, I wasn't too sure what was happening. I think McLaughlin's on very firm ground. His scales…he practices all his scales, the Indian ones, as well. It's really nice to hear a good guitar player playing acoustically in that style. I once thought I'd become as good as that, but I often wonder now whether I've settled down or not.

Yes. Try not to tap your feel too loudly when you're playing, try to move your feet inside your shoes instead of up and down on the floor. It's so irritating when you're trying to hear.

Q.   Does it have any physical effect?

A.   Yes, it does. It makes the guitar move. It alters the comfort and accuracy of the fingering position.

Q.   I found that it interfered with my sense of rhythm.

A.   Yes, it does both occasionally. That's why I try and move my feet inside my shoes. Sometimes I just manage to stick my foot out and just move it backwards and forwards like that, instead of up and down. If I think about it too much, I forget. It's rather like the harder you try to remember the next verse, the more certain you are to forget it. You have to be a bit of a blank. I don't think, as I used to, that I'm a hell of a fellow. I used to think I was a damned interesting sort of a bod, but I don't think so anymore.

Well, there's a world of difference between what I call a free-hand folk style and including clawhammer and the classic approach. I'm really still trying to blend the two of them together. It's very difficult, really. I play less of steel strings than I used to do. I started to feature a few classical pieces in my repertoire now. I feel the good thing about that is it's what people want. They like individuals and ragtime, but also like a great deal of variety in their solo musicians. So I try and give people variety.

Q. There's the argument of sticking with one thing and doing it really well.

A. Yes, there is that, obviously; and I began to feel that the classic style had something to offer me after 16 years of playing free hand without reading music. I learned to read music rather slowly. I still don't read at sight. I'm fairly slow to pick up new things.

Q. Do you think it's important?

A. I don't know. The Buddhists say there are as many paths as there are people; as many paths to heaven as there are people. It's rather like that. Some guitar players rest their little finger on the table of the guitar while they are playing. Which is actually bad because the movement of the third finger is severely impeded by that. If one started with the classical technique, there is no reason why one shouldn't occasionally learn pieces by ear and then write them down. Of course, music was played before it was written. It's bad history to insist on a classical style. This is something I feel upon that very few guitarists would agree. I feel it's very much a matter of individual practice.

Q. Have you played with a plectrum?

A. I have. I found it difficult to play the sort of things I wanted to play that involved playing on alternate strings. John Williams explained it rather well the other evening on TV on the Parkinson Show. "You must play adjacent strings or damp the adjacent strings to the ones you are playing if you use a plectrum." Joe Pass is an interesting example of a good guitar player because he keeps his plectrum in his mouth. He actually uses fingerstyle as well as plectrum playing. Jim Hall's my favorite, though, of the electric players. Kessel's got a fearsome technique.

Q. You have played electric guitar?

A. Yes, I have. I don't think I've realized as many possibilities if I could drive a car. I feel slightly inferior because I don't drive, but I'm just being honest about it. I'd play different instruments more often because I would be able to drive them to gigs. I'm a bit nervous about traveling in cars, anyway.

Q. Any of the younger musicians that you admire?

A. Particularly the Irish ones on the folk scene. Dick Gaughan, the Scot, is a really good player. He has really got those Scottish snaps off to a tee with the plectrum style of playing. Paul Brady is another good example. In the jazz field, I don't know. Quite a lot of jazz players don't have a lot to do with folk clubs, really. I've been off the scene perhaps too much. My feelings about blues are still pretty solid. I'm Muddy Waters oriented now because comparatively few people — unless they're my generation — have records by Broonzy, Lonnie Johnson, or Blind Lemon Jefferson. I'm a terribly lazy person. I think I ought to admit that.

FORTY-TON PARACHUTE

By Davey Graham

LASHTAL'S ROOM

By Davey Graham

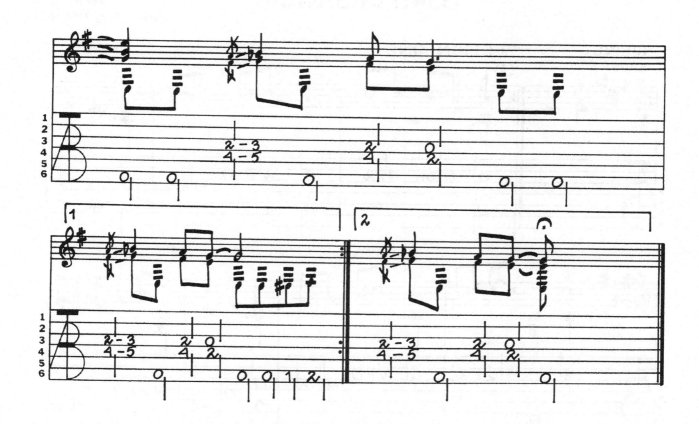

Davey Graham

LORD INCHIQUIN

Traditional
Arr. Davey Graham

LORD MAYO

Traditional
Arr. Davey Graham

Davey Graham

HARDIMAN THE FIDDLER

Traditional
Arr. Davey Graham

THE FAIRIES' HORNPIPE

Traditional
Arr. Davey Graham

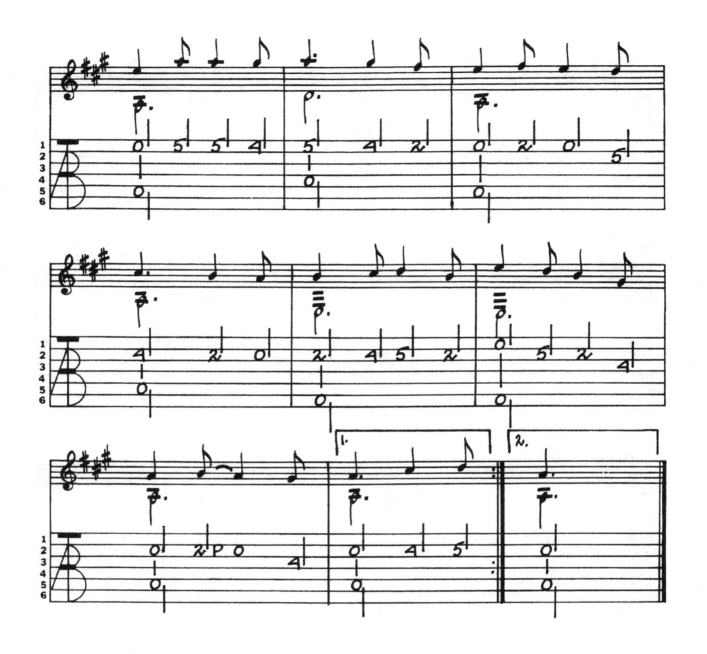

Davey Graham

Photo by Stefan Grossman

Bert Jansch

Photo by Eddie Babbage

BERT JANSCH

Q. Can you tell me, first of all, where and when you were born?

A. In Glasgow, Scotland, in 1943.

Q. When did you first pick up a guitar?

A. Well, that's hard to say, because I'd been trying to make them since I was five years old.

Q. Trying to *make* guitars? What gave you the idea to make guitars?

A. I always wanted one, and I couldn't afford one — so the only way, I thought, was to try and make one. I used to get sheets of hardboard, bits of wood, and cut it all out.

Q. And did you ever succeed in making a guitar?

A. Yeah, when I was about twelve or something, really for real. I honestly actually managed to get one that was reasonably playable.

Q. And that you played on?

A. I learned to play D on it.

Q. And how long did you play that guitar?

A. Not for long. It fell apart eventually. I didn't really play a guitar until I left school at sixteen — a real guitar.

Q. That's when you bought a guitar; and, from the age of five on, who were the guitarists that were influencing you? Why did you want to play a guitar?

A. It wasn't so much the guitar. Lonnie Donnegan was about my first influence into the whole world of music.

Q. When you were sixteen, though, was it still Lonnie Donnegan?

A. No, no that was when I went to a folk club in Scotland — Archie Fisher used to run this club with Jill Doyle, Davey Graham's sister, and obviously I fell madly in love with Jill Doyle when I was sixteen years old, and she used to give guitar lessons, so that's how I got involved.

Q. Was Archie Fisher a major influence in Scotland at that time?

A. He still is. He's a highly respected folk musician, but he used to play all sorts of little pieces of guitar that he'd never actually do on stage. He taught me all the little clawhammer and all those sort of things. Also Len Partridge, have you ever heard of Len Partridge? He's from Scotland. He's a sort of bluesy-type singer, player — really excellent. But he's never performed in public before, so if you're ever up there....

Q. And how long did you stay up in Scotland?

A. I started coming down to London when I was about seventeen — eighteen.

Q. Is that when you met Davey Graham?

A. I honestly can't say when I did actually meet Davey. I think I was a bit older than that, but I knew him through his sister, and she used to have tapes of him ,and I was playing "Angie" when I was about sixteen — fifteen or sixteen. Actually, I was the one that introduced it to Scotland because, from the tapes, no one could work out how to do it until I hit the secret of it all, which was very simple.

Q. Were you only being influenced then by Archie Fisher, Jill Doyle, and Davey Graham's music?

A. ...Les Partridge and also Hamish Imlach. He plays a little bit of bluesy-type stuff.

Q. But no jazz. You weren't listening to jazz music at that time at all?

A. No, I got into that when I came down to London and first started smoking and all that sort of stuff, y'know.

Q. At the age of sixteen you started to take trips down to London. Were you performing in Scotland during this period?

A. No, not really. I mean I first taught the guitar. I didn't actually perform. I used to teach folk guitar to students in Edinburgh because Jill left to go and live in Glasgow, so there was no one to teach the guitar after she left.

Q. So when did you begin to play — think that you could do it as a professional musician — performing-wise?

A. I got drunk one night and actually sang. That was when I was about seventeen — all the actual dates are very vague to me.

Q. When did you start composing and writing instrumentals and songs?

A. Almost as soon as I picked up the guitar. I wrote my first song, "Green Are Your Eyes," when I was about sixteen.

Q. Your first Transatlantic record — how old were you when you made that?

A. Nineteen, twenty.

Q. When did you establish yourself down in London, then?

A. It was prior to the album coming out. I think the first club I did was The King and Queen, which was a pub in Soho. Also, The Troubador. I remember doing the Troubador because Bob Dylan did it the week before I did. The girl that ran the club remarked on the similarity of, not the music, but the approach to our presenting the music.

Q. At that period of time, who were the musicians you were hanging out with and who were affecting your music both in London and Scotland?

A. Clive Palmer, Robin Williamson. Not Archie 'cause Archie was very loathe to come down to London. He didn't want to leave Scotland, but we used to share a flat together up in Scotland. Me and Clive and Robin, and out of that came The Incredible String Band!

Q. So when did the Davey Graham, John Renbourn, Bert Jansch....

A. ...Syndrome! Good word! I knew Davey all the years up to the point where I met you. I'd actually lived with John for years so that we were very close musically and thought-wise. But Davey was always a very lone-type figure — a very mysterious figure. Even today he still is. Why people should put our names together — I've got no idea. I can understand putting me and John together because we actually worked together, and we brought out an album together, and stuff like that — but why there should be three names, I've got no idea. Maybe it was just simply because I was so influenced by Davey.

Q. In which way were you influenced by Davey?

A. Just the technique. Just watching him a couple of times, you know. Also, "Angie" because every time I play a guitar, I always play "Angie."

Q. But technique-wise you are very different.

A. Our techniques are very different, but I did learn a lot from him. He used to play tunes like Charlie Menevs' "Better Get It in Your Soul," and I do a number which is taken directly from that.

Q. At this period of time you were nineteen, twenty, and were starting to smoke and listen to Charles Lloyd, Mingus, Coltrane, and other jazz figures. How did their music affect your approach to playing the guitar?

A. Well, it got me out of the guitar itself and realizing that a lot of good music is not played on the guitar. It's actually played on other instruments, and that's how it affected me.

Q. How about American guitar players at that time? Rev. Davis and Jack Elliot were very popular here. Was their music affecting you at all?

A. No, not one bit, funnily enough! As a guitarist, I was never influenced by American playing. I mean, the clawhammer techniques I learned. I learned in Scotland, and I learned them from Scotsmen who had already gone through all that. The American players that I heard were Brownie McGhee, Big Bill Broonzy, Leadbelly, and Woody Guthrie. They were the mainstay for me at that time. All the others came later. Even Snooks Eaglin came a long time later. I realize that he was a great influence on Davey Graham. In actual fact, a lot of Davey's playing is very similar. All those people came later — even Mississippi John Hurt was much later, Blind Blake, even — all these people.

Q. Of the three — Renbourn, Graham, Jansch — yours is the most, to me, "British" playing. I don't hear very much American influences except maybe with a few jazz tunes you play.

A. That might have come from my delving into just jazz things, like Charlie Mingus and people like that — John Coltrane.

Q. What I'm talking about, specifically, your right-hand technique, your technique for arranging, the actual playing, your arranging of a ballad. And I see that all in the "school" of Archie Fisher, Martin Carthy, Bert Jansch. There's something very British happening there.

A. I think I created it, actually.

Q. You think you created that? When did Martin Carthy start to get into the picture?

A. About the same time.

Q. But do you feel that he was or is doing something that you're doing, similar?

A. No, I think he was influenced in a way that you could actually do things like that on a guitar. It's like, I think "The Blackwaterside" — the version I do of that was the earliest song I'd ever attempted which was an English traditional song. I learned that from Anne Briggs, who is a traditional singer.

Q. You learned the song from Anne Briggs, not the playing?

A. Oh, no, no — that was just my arrangement of the song.

Q. So we're trying to pin something that is very ethereal — which is important. I don't know if we can pin it down. How did you go about getting into that sound? Was it anything conscious? Because it is a very distinct approach that has affected guitar playing.

A. I think in many ways it was consciously done. I think it may have been one of the first times that I had actually sat down and tried to take a number instead of writing a song or writing an instrumental or doing something with that, but rather to take a number that had a definite melody line that I couldn't change — it's a traditional thing — and actually consciously sit down and create a backing to go with that particular tune. I've never, ever done that before. I had written songs like "Green Are Your Eyes" or played an instrumental or sung a blues, but this was the first time I'd ever actually sat down and taken a folk song other than a Woody Guthrie-type song.

Q. But, thinking back, the arrangement that came out for that tune — where do you think the roots lie? You say it's something you created.

A. Well, I think all the roots were just generally what I'd been doing before — the instrumentals, particularly Davey Graham.

Q. I think also your playing is very different from John's, Davey's, and Archie's. The way to attack the "strings" is very unique.

A. "Attack" them is the right word!

Q. What's the story with your hands?

A. Well, they're pretty big!

Q. No, I was told you had problems with your hands — you have a rheumatism of the hands.

A. It's not rheumatism. It's arthritis, and it's incurable, really. I can only play a certain amount before my wrists and joints seize up. So therefore, believe it or not, I very rarely practice anything — so it's difficult — and it's been like that for five or six years.

Q. When you play, is it generally with your thumbnail and the balls of your index and middle fingers?

A. Yes, I use these three.

Q. Oh, also the ring finger; but using the balls of your fingers or your nails?

A. Both. You can see a slight callous there and then it catches on the nail, but I can't play without the nail.

Q. That snapping effect that you get — in America we would relate it to the Mississippi Delta — but you wouldn't.... It had nothing to do with that. Where did you get into that?

A. Just sheer aggression!

Q. There was no one doing it before you? It was just a sound that you liked?

A. It wasn't the sound so much as you'd be playing in a club, and if the club was noisy you were trying to get as much out of the strings as possible. In the old days, I used to actually break the strings, I'd get so angry.

Q. But you started to use the effect in your arrangements?

A. Right, because it became a sort of dynamic effect.

Q. Going back now, we have you living with John Renbourn, being affected by Archie Fisher, Clive Palmer, and Robin Williamson, and then where did you go from there?

A. Well, that was the lead-up to The Pentangle. John and I had been living together two or three years or more, and we decided to get a club together, basically just for the two of us. You know, that's what I don't understand about folk singers nowadays. I don't see the young people starting a club just so they can play, let alone anything else.

Q. Before you started the club, though, there was a period when you were involved with Donovan, or Donovan was involved with you, and there was Derrol Adams.

A. Well, that was the early days of the Les Cousins Club. I did a residency in a place called The Scots House, which you may know of.... It's now changed names, I think. And also a residency in Les Cousins. I used to do one on a Tuesday and one on a Thursday, which was highly improbable to do such a thing, to actually have two residencies 50 yards apart in the same week, but it used to work. Donovan used to come down. I didn't really know him very well, but he used to come down, and around that time Derrol Adams was hanging around. They got involved as people and slowly I got involved, as well.

Q. Yet Donovan sort of used your music.

A. It was just a passing thing, though obviously he was very famous at the time, which to everyone in folk clubs was very...you know, the awe and the wonder of it all to actually know someone that had been on television!

Q. But he seemed to have been affected by your music.

A. He was affected by everything that was going on at the time. There was also another guy called Jackson C. Frank, and he had a lot of influence with a lot of people, for some strange unreal reason.

Q. So we got to where you start The Horseshoe Club with John, and then what happens?

A. John and I were starting to think about bands at that point. We're thinking, "Let's get a band together," do something.

Q. Whereas John's achievements, recording-wise, up until then had generally just been making records of English versions of American tunes — American blues, American folk song. He hadn't really found his style yet, or anything uniquely his.

A. No, he didn't. He was...that's when he got into the sort of Medieval type.

Q. …Which was after?

A. …Just slightly. That was the beginning of it, though. We were always reading things like *Morte d' Arthur* and things like that…delving back into very old literature. But I suppose in that way he got involved in listening to all the music of those periods at the same time.

Q. How did you get together with Terry Cox, Danny Thompson, and Jacqui McShee to form The Pentangle?

A. John was doing a show called *Gadzooks! It's All Happening,* a TV show with Julie Felix. This was how all this ties up, you see. Danny was backing Julie, I think, and Terry, and I can't remember if John was involved. I think it was something to do with Doris Henderson. She was on the show, as well, if I remember. Anyway, that's how they all introduced each other. I had no part in all this, and John invited them all to the club. So after that they just…took over. We spent a whole year doing that club and The Pentangle was formed, and the first gig we did after that was The Festival Hall, which we sold out — no publicity, nothing, just virtually taking all the people that had come to the club and putting them into The Festival Hall!

Q. And with The Pentangle itself as a musical experiment — a musical experience — how did you feel about it?

A. I think it was great. I learned a lot about people mainly, traveled around the world.

Q. And your music itself — was it able to grow within that experience?

A. Not on my own, no. In fact, it was quite retarded. I was able to put out a couple of albums, one being *Rosemary Lane,* while the band was still going. There was one prior to that which I didn't like very much — *Birthday Blues*. But no, I learned a lot about musicians — other people, other musicians — through that, but it also restricted us in a lot of ways. But I loved it! I thought it was great.

Q. And that disbanded after how many years?

A. Six or seven.

Q. That long? And now you're getting back to playing solo again in the last years. You and the guitar. Your records are getting more involved with you as the songwriter.

A. I think I'm a pretty good songwriter, but people don't seem to take much notice of it! I think I'm a better songwriter than I am a guitarist. Guitar playing has a limit.

Q. But your guitar playing is very, very unique.

A. Well, it's unique, but it still has its limit, you know. I don't think it'll go beyond a certain stage.

Q. But I think in a different way it has. Your arrangement of "Blackwaterside" has been recorded by Led Zeppelin on their first record. Jimmy Page copied it directly. This is an example of your guitar style starting to reach a bigger audience.

A. On that album it's called "Black Mountainside."

Q. When I first met you, you were using a John Bailey guitar, but you stopped using that?

A. No, it got nicked!

Q. Did you like that guitar?

A. The first one, yes; but the second one he built for me wasn't the same. It had a different feel.

Q. But they were essentially copies of the Martin 000-28. Why was that?

A. You see, up to the point that I had that guitar made, I didn't actually own one. The first one I had when I left school when I was about sixteen. I bought this Lonnie Donnegan guitar which was really great! I really loved it! It's actually a Zenith guitar. It used to be called a Josh White guitar, then it was changed to Lonnie Donnegan, but it was a great little guitar. That got nicked when I was about seventeen. Ever since then I've been borrowing guitars. On my first album there's about three or four different guitars on it, none of them mine.

Q. But on the cover it's you with a...?

A. Oh, that's Les Bridges' guitar. Les Bridges was a guy that John and I used to live with.

Q. Was that a 000-28 Martin?

A. That was a 000-28, so that when I had the John Bailey guitar made, I said look — I want it to be like this one. I had a copy made of it. The next one was a bit of an experiment of his own ideas, which didn't really quite work; but all my guitars have been similar to the Martin 000-28. I've actually owned a Martin since then, which I traded in for a Japanese guitar.

Q. It's a Yamaha, right? You set it up with light-gauge strings.

A. Yes.

Q. So it's a triple-0 body guitar, 14-fret, set up with light-gauge strings. These are a guitar player's questions.

A. When I was working with Pentangle, I put extra-light on because you're working so much that it was often just sheer physical hard work to actually play. So I used to put on extra-light.

Q. And you were also playing 12-string? You used to go on stage with a 12- and a 6-?

A. Right, but I gave that up because it was too much of a hustle. Also, I gave the guitar to Wizz Jones. That 12-string was a John Bailey — it was a beautiful 12-string.

Bert Jansch

Photo Courtesy of May Management

BLACK WATERSIDE

Traditional
Arr. Bert Jansch

56

57

ALICE'S WONDERLAND

By Bert Jansch

59

REPEAT
FROM THE
TOP TO ⊕ SIGN

THEN PLAY
⊕ CODA BELOW

VERONICA

By Bert Jansch

(OPTIONAL RETURN TO B HERE)

D.C.

65

THE WHEEL

By Bert Jansch

nb: Stems in the music indicate upper and lower voices. Tab stems indicate thumb or finger.

repeat and fade...

72

ST. FIACRE'S REVENGE

By Bert Jansch

74

Bert Jansch

BRIDGE

By Bert Jansch
and Martin Jenkins

Bert Jansch

John Renbourn

Photo by Stefan Grossman

JOHN RENBOURN

Q. Can you tell me when you first began to pick up the guitar?

A. I first began playing when skiffle was a craze in England, Chas McDevitt, Lonnie Donegan, Dickie Bishop, and an American who was over here called Johnny Duncan. There used to be radio broadcasts regularly of a thing called The Skiffle Club, or Skiffle Cellar, and I think that's probably the first time I heard wire-strung guitars being played. In fact, that was the first time I became aware of guitar at all. That and the beginning of pop music in England, so far as I remember, which is the breakthrough on television of programs like the *Six Five Special,* one later on called *Oh Boy,* which the British equivalent to American stars, Tommy Steele, and that sort of thing. I must have been about 13 or 14 at the time (1959).

Q. And what part of England were you living in?

A. Around south London. And, as you know, what happened then was that a lot of the songs that people were interested in, skiffle songs, turned out to be Leadbelly songs. Just about that time, there was also the revival in folk music and there were broadcasts from the Singers Club, which used to have quite a lot of American players. Rory McKuen published a book called *How to Play Folk Guitar.* It's a long time ago. I showed Woody Guthrie licks, scratch, picking different sorts of things. I became interested in the mysteries of who these various people were. Who was Big Bill Broonzy?! Just about the same time Jack Elliot was over. I think that he was probably amazingly important in the fact that, after that, a lot of people were playing fingerpicking or flatpicking and fingerpicking of a simple nature, based mainly on Jack Elliot's style. That's going forward a bit, but that's when I first started to take an interest in it. And then, of course, after that there were a lot of people playing mixtures of black American music, very much like the kind of stuff that's in my repertoire now.

Q. And at that period of time then in the English scene, the influence was clearly an American guitar style?

A. Absolutely! Totally! I mean, the repertoire was "Cocaine," "San Francisco Bay Blues," just about everything from the 10" LP *Jack Takes the Floor* by Jack Elliot. Jessie Fuller records started to come in, Broonzy records were available, it was also the beginning of the trad jazz. In fact, the skiffle thing actually was a branch of the traditional jazz-band stuff, and then there was a revived interest in all sorts of folk music. And then there was a big kind of split between English and American, and guitars were very much out in folk clubs, and most of the good players in fact would never have gone into a folk club, anyway. It's a very oppressive attitude towards music. It was all to do with English music for the English type of thing. Well, you still find it today, of course, you know.

Q. Well, your guitar playing then — you started off just basing it on American styles, and you were an amateur.

A. Right, but American styles learned from other people who in fact probably half learned them themselves, you know. Of which there were, in fact, quite a large number of players around.

Q. At what age, then, did you begin being an amateur to a semi-professional to a professional musician?

A. I was never a professional musician until I came out of art school and then found that that was, more or less, the only way I could make any money. By then I was actually doing quite a lot of folk clubs, anyway. I was about 19 then.

Q. And playing by yourself or with other people, performing-wise?

A. No, I used to play with another guy who played 12-string, and before that I used to jam with quite a few people doing duets and things. All American stuff.

Q. So when did the London scene happen with you, Bert Jansch, Doris Henderson, and Jackie McShee? What period of time in relation to your development?

A. Well, at the time I was at art school, I met a 12-string player called Chris Aliff who teamed up with Jacqui, and then I met Jacqui and Bert, more or less, at the same time. Even before that, I heard of Davey Graham.

Q. And this is when they were still up in Scotland?

A. I think Bert had just sort of, more or less, come down to London by then.

Q. And was Davey Graham an influence on you at that period?

A. Yes. At that time Davey was playing with John Mayall in a sort of pick-up R&B band. He was playing a Gibson with a pick-up, and he was the first person I'd seen using bass lines played in sixths, which of course a lot of people play now. In fact, playing harmony parts on the guitar as a back-up for R&B-type music. And I was also playing in a little R&B-type band, as well, which was doing Jimmy Reed-type things.

Q. When did you get together with Bert?

A. I'm trying to think.... There were a number of clubs in London. The Roundhouse had reopened. There was a night place called The Student Prince, Bunjies, and The Scots House, which Bert used to have a residency in. And I met Doris Henderson when she came to The Roundhouse, and this was possibly the first time I'd ever played blues with somebody who actually knew how to sing blues or had some kind of blues upbringing. Her father was a preacher. In fact, the first record I did was with Doris, which was an album which had, it was just the two of us, a number of things like "Going to Memphis." She was singing and playing autoharp. Paul Simon, by the way, came over round about that time as well and, in fact, Bert by then had written a lot of excellent songs that were way beyond the type of thing that most people like myself were attempting to play. I certainly wasn't into the stage of creating anything at that point, you know.

Q. And was Paul part of the circle of friends?

A. Paul used to play at the Student Prince and down in Bunjies and a few other places. I think that was like a huge boost, particularly for the type of songwriters that were around there when he came over. I think he and Bert knew each other fairly well, anyway, and I think they both had a certain amount of influence on each other.

Q. At that period, Bert Jansch was in the vanguard of guitar players who were also writing songs?

A. I think he was certainly the best. Way beyond the best, you know! He was creating things that were definitely new. Certainly new so far as I was concerned.

Q. And Davey Graham, what was his influence at that time?

A. Well, everybody knew everybody else. Davey and Bert knew each other. Of course, the LP with "Angie" on was, I suppose, the starting point for lots of people to play a type of music that wasn't strongly American influenced. Davey himself was another guy that tried to put his own music concepts, which were in fact huge by comparison to most people's — North African music, Indian music, jazz, folk-style playing, blues, and just every kind of influence imaginable — into his playing. I think at that point he was certainly the most adventurous player.

Q. So he was the most adventuresome, whereas Bert was doing more creatively?

A. Yes, Bert was writing songs and instrumentals which were very much his own type of thing, although it came, I guess, based on picking styles. We used some clawhammer playing, variations on thumb patterns, but way beyond the standard chords associated with country playing — Doc Watson-type things. But Davey was far more varied, I think, in the type of music he played. At that time there was another record that Davey made with a tune called "She Moved Through the Fair." I've heard him play that tune taking it completely out of context, even in those days, and using harmonics played behind the frets. Very fine playing, you know.

Q. People talk of Davey's "Angie" being a popular tune, but they always talk of "She Moved Through the Fair" as being a turning point in the approach to English guitar playing. To Martin Carthy and Bert Jansch, it seems to be that tune which represented the first step in how English people could play an English style. Do you feel that, too?

A. Yes, very likely it was. But Davey did actually instill us into playing English music in a way. He made a record with Shirley Collins which you probably know, *New Roots, Folk Roots,* which split the folk world. A lot of people thought it was very fine — I certainly did — and a lot of people thought that it was a very wrong approach to the music. Just after that, Bert made a record called *Jack Orion.* I suppose it could be traced maybe back to the way Davey was playing "She Moved Through the Fair," but nevertheless taken in a far more personal way using, in fact, a dropped D and a lot of little rolling phrases, elaborate playing but based on folk, traditional singing stylings. The grace notes, which were considered very important, and people were in fact teaching ornamentation in folk singing, unaccompanied folk singing. Anne Briggs knew Bert, and I think Bert learned a number of good tunes from her which he then found that the ornaments could be played on the guitar. That became labelled the "folk baroque." Do you remember? Karl Dallas or somebody named it that, mainly because the guitar style appeared very elaborate at that point, way beyond the traditional idea that if you were going to use the guitar at all it should be very subordinate.

Q. Tell me about your getting together with Bert, starting to play together, and your influences on each other, as well as your alienation from the folk world.

A. Let's think.... Well, one of the places we lived in was a house where downstairs Royston Wood and Peter Bellamy lived, and we used to live upstairs. Les Bridges, Bert, and myself.

Q. Had you gotten to know Bert in the club scene?

A. Yes, that's right. I think I met Bert probably in either the Roundhouse or Bunjies. At that time, I think I was playing guitar for Doris, and she was also going around playing the London clubs, and Bert was doing much the same sort of thing. I don't actually clearly remember meeting him on any specific occasion. I know that I knew other people that we were all friendly with, guys called Hennessey and Wizz Jones. There was a club called The Black Horse, which was probably the main point, that was in Rathbone Place. There was a very active folk scene then. Alex Campbell was doing a lot. Peter Sayers, Long John Baldry, and Malcome Price were all performing.

Q. You got friendly with Bert, friendly enough to live together, in other words.

A. I think what happened was I was looking for a place to live and Les, who I was friendly with as well, said there was a place going, and we all moved into this one room. I found that there was very little conscious effort of working out tunes with Bert or attempting to play tunes for a project or anything like that. A lot of the music came together just because it was the type of scene where various people came in to play, and I happened to play occasionally, and Bert was there. A lot of music went on, and I think we worked out some tunes, one of which was called "Lucky Thirteen," a song that Doris used to sing that Bert learned a little riff from, and we played that and it became an instrumental. I think that was probably the first instrumental I did which was on a record of Bert's (Bert's second record). I played guitar on some of his songs, and I found it very easy to make music with Bert inasmuch as he's so easy-going when he's putting some music together and that it's very enjoyable. It's almost the state where you could actually play anything together. In actual fact, you don't play anything but there is very little pressure on the type of music. We also found that we'd frequently have bits of tunes which would either, for some strange coincidence, be in harmony, that two instrumental tunes would actually fit, which is more or less the way that the Bert and John album came about. Or we'd have sections that would become another part of the same tune.

Q. You came into that period of your life starting off being very influenced by American music which had been transmitted to you by second or third generation. Now Bert, at that time, was doing, for want of a better word, a very British type of guitar playing. How did that influence your playing?

A. The first time I heard Bert, I just couldn't imagine what on earth he was doing. I didn't recognize the shapes. I liked it. I was astounded by it! Even working with him in Pentangle there was a lot of things that I just didn't know what they were. So that was pretty astounding.

Q. And at that period of time, when you began to play together, you got alienated from the British folk-club scene. Why was that?

A. Well, I think by that time there were certain people running clubs that in fact were trying to keep tradition revived and were pushing a very heavy traditional line. It was bad, it was very bad from that point of view. It didn't actually worry me too much because I wasn't too anxious to force it on anyone.

Q. So as a result of that period, you think of yourself as a musician playing music. You play folk songs to jazz tunes to original tunes, not as an exponent of British folk music.

A. Not at all, no. But for a long time I didn't play any traditional music, mainly because it was more or less felt that I was unable to. Even now I certainly don't regard the traditional tunes I play as being the best way of playing them. I just do them because I enjoy the tunes. The tunes are very strong, very interesting to harmonize, and I just enjoy it.

Q. Your first two records on Transatlantic were records of American folk tunes. You were singing and playing the guitar. At the same time Pentangle formed, you did two or three records which have Renaissance music and jazz tunes. Were you conscious of that complete about-face?

A. Early music was something I'd always been interested in, but it had got to the point when the guitar playing had become so elaborate that it became difficult to play all the ideas on one instrument. I started to think in terms of separate lines, which is something that is a very good approach to guitar playing. If you're attempting to write something and you've got an idea for an instrumental, try and separate how many parts it falls into. Generally, it's like a separate bass and a separate melody, which is a step away from the picking style, which is like an alternate bass. It's more like a single-line thing. This is particularly like the way Bert plays "Blackwaterside," for example. There's a tune and a bass line, but they both fit very well on the guitar. I think I was anxious to keep the lines and perhaps restrict the guitar playing to, say, two lines and then maybe have recorders or another instrument playing a separate line. I started to put some things together, one of them was a tune, a thing called

"Morgana," which is on the *John Alot* record, which was an extension to thinking about guitar, but using other instruments to play the lines.

Q. At that same period you were with the group The Pentangle. How did The Pentangle get together?

A. Well, that was another pretty loose thing. Bert and I were playing a bit, and I was doing some things with Jacqui at the same time at The Cousins, Danny and Terry were playing with Alexis Korner, and I think we sort of decided maybe we'd start a club ourselves and Bert would play and I'd do some things on my own and do some things with Jacqui, and we'd finish off the evening with Danny and Terry. There was no huge scheme involved. Just to start a band, you know.

Q. There was a scheme on Bert's side, wasn't there? I mean, he really wanted to have a band at that period.

A. Well maybe. He'd done a record called *Nicola*, which is a very orchestrated record, and a lot of his songs were given a big treatment, and I think in a way he probably liked the idea of putting forward his songs using other musicians.

Q. That whole period of The Pentangle, how did you feel about it?

A. Well, that again was like a big boost when it first started, particularly for me. Working with Danny and Terry was excellent for me. In a group the music has to be more analyzed, and I found that very fine.

Q. Was there any tension?

A. Well, certainly not at the beginning because it was so new for all of us. It was probably the first time that Danny and Terry had ever come in touch with anything remotely like folk music, which of course they'd always been highly skeptical of and thought that it was like a form of music that was for the illiterates and in fact not music at all. I guess that they were impressed by the type of songs that Bert was writing and the fact that they did have a lot of interesting time changes in the, and the accent shifted a great deal and they were fine. Bert's style is based on so many things. Bert in fact was doing Charlie Mingus-type tunes. So the group more or less started with the idea that we could perhaps find a common ground.

Q. How did it end? Did it get frustrating for you?

A. Well, it grew far larger than it was ever intended to be. It was just intended to be a little thing to play Sunday nights, and it wound up being a big touring band, and there were a lot of huge business problems, and a lot of hard work, particularly doing the tours of the States and Australia. There were a lot of pressures on us that had nothing to do with the actual creation of the music and very little to do with putting the music across. We were eventually playing stadiums with people like The Grateful Dead, Canned Heat, and big American rock bands, all kinds of stuff and it was no fun whatsoever.

Q. But the music to the end was satisfying. You didn't feel that your creativity was being stifled by the format?

A. Well, nobody was under any obligation to restrict themselves to the group. Although, of course, towards the end we were working so much there was no time to do anything else. I think everyone started to think they were spending too much time playing with the group and not enough time making their own music. It became like a fixed unit, which it was never intended to be. Plus the fact that we were all living in different places. Terry was living in Spain, Bert was living in Wales, I was living somewhere else, that it just became very difficult. It just became more a way of going out and not really playing and coming back again. So the music itself stopped, I think, quite some time before the group actually no longer existed.

Q. Do you feel there's any schizophrenic tendency in your musical output on record in that even after that period, after the band disbanded, you put together a record which was folk songs and singing, and your next solo record after that was *The Hermit,* which is all guitar instrumentals going back toward the *Sir John Alot.*

A. That's not exactly right. The point is that I had, with The Pentangle, different agreements, contracts, and what not, and I found I had to do a record for Transatlantic. I also had some songs I was working on which I wanted to do which Warner Bros. never released, so in fact there was a record in between *Faro Annie* and *The Hermit* which never saw the light of day. But the reason that *The Hermit* took so long was because of all the contractual problems left over when the group split up.

Q. *The Hermit* represents the next progression from *Sir John Alot* and *The Lady and the Unicorn.*

A. Well, it does and it doesn't. It represents the fact that I was working, or in fact living, in the same area as Tony Roberts, the flute player. Sue Draheim was living there. And Tony played on *The Lady and the Unicorn,* and I had the idea of putting together a type of music that combined the Elizabethan-type music with Sue playing country fiddle and possibly having another small group. Contractually, it became possible to record again, and the record company specifically wanted a solo record to start with. So I decided it would be best to make a purely instrumental record and possibly to use the group as a little nucleus.

Q. You were influenced by a whole wide spectrum of music. Can you talk about that?

A. Well, there's a huge repertoire of lute music, some of which can be played on the guitar. And even if the pieces themselves can't be played on the guitar, it's possible to use the type of construction or the way of thinking that made the lute music and play that on the guitar. I think the most enjoyable approach is to regard the guitar as a keyboard instrument with the possibility of playing the separate parts, rather than embracing a style of playing which you then have to fit all the music into. My style now borders more on a classical approach to the guitar, I think. Do you not agree? Some of the things on *The Hermit* could well be played on classical guitar.

Q. What I think is curious, though, is that your influences are lute music, classical music, jazz, country blues. I think that's fascinating someone can play a tune by Skip James, and the next moment play a John Dowland lute piece. It's rather unusual to find someone who has interests in such a vast array of music.

A. Well, I don't find that unusual. I see no reason that music, that any good music, should be separated or that people should in fact become specialists. I think that's extremely bad.

Q. I agree. What I'm trying to find out is who's influenced John Renbourn?

A. Well, I listen to a great deal of music without thinking of it as being an influence on me, and it ranges right the way from people I know who play to, I don't know, I'm interested in Guillaume de Machaut as a composer, who was writing in the 1300s and using compositional techniques which now have come back into circulation with Stravinsky. But it's a type of music that predates the major-and-minor-scales type of what would be considered modal music, which of course a lot of English and American folk tunes are. And as an approach to harmonizing a folk tune, it's already been in early music considered all the way right from the parallel harmonies right through to the beginning of counterpoint. But some of his pieces are just excellent — "William Byrd," of course. Do you know the Virginal Book, *Fitzwilliam Virginal Book?* Very fine if you're interested in English part writing, but in say four-part writing, which is an approach to any sort of music.

Q. Explain this which is confusing to me: On your records you have completely solo guitar pieces or solo guitar with accompaniment. Yet when you're doing a concert by yourself, 90 percent of it is you singing and playing, and maybe you play one or two instrumentals.

A. Well, I actually enjoy singing and playing, but I certainly don't do it particularly well. The singing aspect is dreadful! But if people are prepared to stand for it, that's very fine.

Q. Why aren't you playing so many instrumentals on stage?

A. Generally because the instrumentals that I prepared for my solo albums are mindbenders. None of them are easy to play. None of them, in fact, allow for anything ever to go wrong. There's no room for improvisation in any of them, whereas a lot of the instrumentals I used to play were a bit of a constructed tune followed by more or less an improvisation, not freely improvised, but nevertheless with a lot of stock phrases that may or may not be used depending on how I felt. I seem to have gone away from that type of playing, and it takes a lot of bravery on my part to attempt any of these set pieces, is what it's down to.

Q. You're just reluctant that you might make mistakes, and the domino theory, the whole piece would just fall down on you.

A. Yes, once the tune collapses of that nature, there's just no way of picking them up again. It's just laziness on my part. I'm quite happy to have recorded the tunes, very pleased to have actually worked them out and possibly put them in a book of some sort. But I think if I was going to do a special concert then I would no doubt get down to really getting down to work again. They're far harder to play than anything I've done in the past.

Q. Your guitar technique is, I think, worth talking about. Whereas most of the folk-orientated people play with a heavy hand, for want of a better word, you're using a steel-strung guitar with very light-gauge strings and playing almost in a classical position, using classical techniques. How did that develop? Is that a conscious development?

A. I used to play, or have, a nylon guitar way back before I even had a steel-string guitar that was playable. I got into playing the guitar with steel strings when I was hitchhiking around and just keeping the guitar with me. I would take that with me. I think for quite some time I would find it easier and more enjoyable to play the nylon-strung guitar, but it's difficult. I mean, do you in fact play classical guitar at all? No, you find that once you do start playing it at first you're not so happy with the things that are coming out of it, and then you find after a while that it's a far more responsive instrument and that the steel-strung guitar sounds very limited in its tone colors. You know, it's a coming and going sort of thing.

Q. Why aren't you playing a nylon-string guitar?

A. Well, I do at home. I've no idea why I don't actually play it on stage (or on record). Yeah, I should do, really.

Q. And what type of guitar are you playing now at home? On stage?

A. A guild D55, a Franklin OM-3A, and a cheap Aria acoustic amplified guitar.

Q. And strung up with what?

A. D'Addario strings: 48 bass, and a 10 top; 48, 38 28, covered 18 for a third, 14 for a second, and 10 for a top. Very light-gauge strings; extra, extra light.

Q. And your nails and the way you strike the guitar are very classically orientated?

A. Yes, I use fingernails. Not quite as long as you would, I think, if you were playing classical guitar.

Q. But the string hits only the nail, or does it hit the ball of your finger?

A. Well, both, really. I think if you use just purely the nail you get a very thin sound. I think it's possibly a combination of the two — I'm not sure. I don't know, I mean, my actual technique is like homemade but it's based on, very loosely, as you say, on a classical right-hand position which of course doesn't work at all if you play blues, so you've got to adapt your hand position. If you want to damp your strings, you have to turn your hand 'round to another position. I'm never really conscious of a position.

Q. But do you find that's a problem? Because that position will work out fine for Elizabethan lute music, but when you're playing a blues it can cause difficulties.

A. Exactly, it more or less ruins you if you're intending to play nothing but classical music. But as I play anything I like, anytime I like, it doesn't really worry me what happens.

Q. Are you conscious also that the end result of this right-hand position has very little to do, if anything, with the original sound and texture of the country blues?

A. No, I'm no longer concerned with actually playing exactly like anyone else. All I'm interested in is the tune which I like and how the tune can be fitted on to the guitar.

Q. Well, do you realize that the end result is a unique sound?

A. Well, I mean, obviously it's different; but I wouldn't class it as anything else except my approach to playing that tune.

Q. I was trying to figure out whether it was just by "default" or whether there was a conscious effort to make a unique sound.

A. No, there's certainly no conscious effort to make a unique sound. I mean, the number of people who attempt to play like me or sound like me probably do it far more than I've ever been concerned about it. My concern is playing the type of music I like; how it actually sounds is an accident.

Q. For someone who is interested in learning how to play the instrument, what type of advice could you give them?

A. Well, there's the obvious advice that, if you in fact do attempt to do things too fast, you'll find that you can in fact get into habits that are later on difficult to extract yourself from. There's one school of thought that says, if you ever use your left hand to play a chord, play all the notes in the chord, even if you're not going to sound them. Which I think can be very bad later on, when you in fact need to use the fingers that you've actually clamped down every time. You have to, in fact, think of not using them, which is difficult. It's probably better to learn very simple things, the type of things that are outlined in the Carcassi books. Any sort of finger exercises are very good. This gives you independence of the fingers of the right hand. Little patterns are very good to play, like just around the C chord using different patterns of the right hand. These, of course, can also be used for song accompaniment. But the other advice, which I think is very good, is don't certainly limit yourself to playing guitar music. Try and play any possible type of music you can. Sheet music is very good, like old standards. Play anything you can get hold of. Even if it's not actually possible to play it on the guitar, play what you can.

Q. So you would recommend that guitar players learn how to read music?

A. Well, that's a difficult one. A lot of great players don't know how to read music. And of course a lot of people with a lot of natural talent would probably find, in fact, that reading music could alter their views so much and it would be very bad for them. It's difficult because a lot of people I know that play very good and elaborate pieces find that, when they actually attempt to read music, the type of things they're playing are so more advanced than the stage they are ever likely to reach studying music that it becomes bad for them. But if you're just beginning, of course, it's a very good idea. You can actually see the music clearly on the paper which, I think, is an aid to understanding the way you play.

Q. I've noticed you had a change of feelings on music notation. Your first book just had music notation for your pieces. It was very much a classical approach to how to play your tunes, whereas your second and third books use music as well as tablature.

A. Well, that in actual fact was because I didn't realize at the time — I forget when I was doing it, more or less when Pentangle was touring — and I was completely out of touch with who was playing guitar and how many guitar players there were around playing good guitar music. It was way before the popularity of ragtime playing, and I really had no idea that 90 percent of them read tablature so well and didn't read music, and so I didn't include tablature in the book. I assumed that if anyone was going to take the trouble to learn tablature they'd probably find it just as easy to learn simple guitar music. But in actual fact, very few guitar players read music.

Q. Which guitar players would you suggest for up-and-coming guitar players to get involved with so far as listening and learning from?

A. I suppose, for extremely good accompaniment, Doc Watson would be a good example. He plays a variety of things; all of them are extremely good music and not all of them at virtuoso level. Some of them are, in fact, playable by people who are just starting. Bert and Davey, of course, Julian Bream and John Williams. I don't know, there are just so many good players.

LADY NOTHYNGE'S TOYE PUFFE

By John Renbourn

John and Jacob Renbourn

Photo by Stefan Grossman

THE MOON SHINES BRIGHT

Traditional
Arr. John Renbourn

REPEAT SECTIONS B AND A

THE HERMIT

By John Renbourn

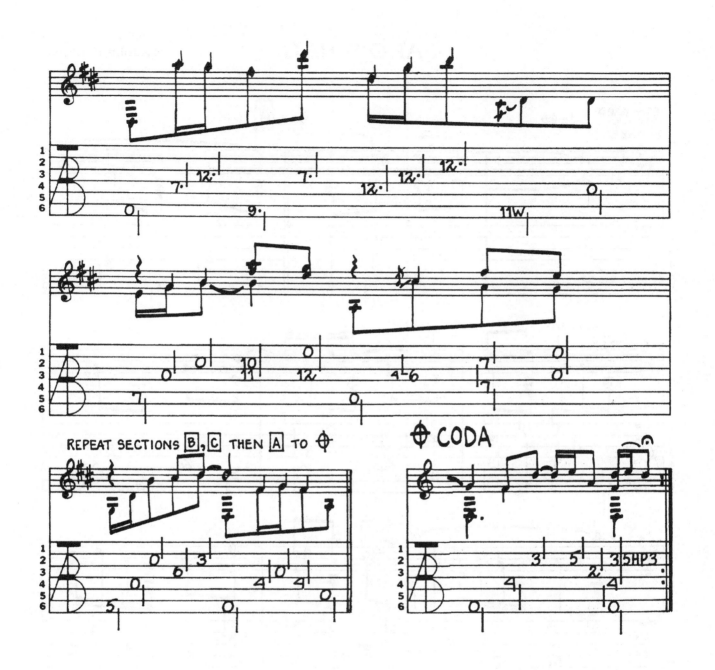

REPEAT SECTIONS B, C THEN A TO ⊕

⊕ CODA

113

FARO'S RAG

By John Renbourn

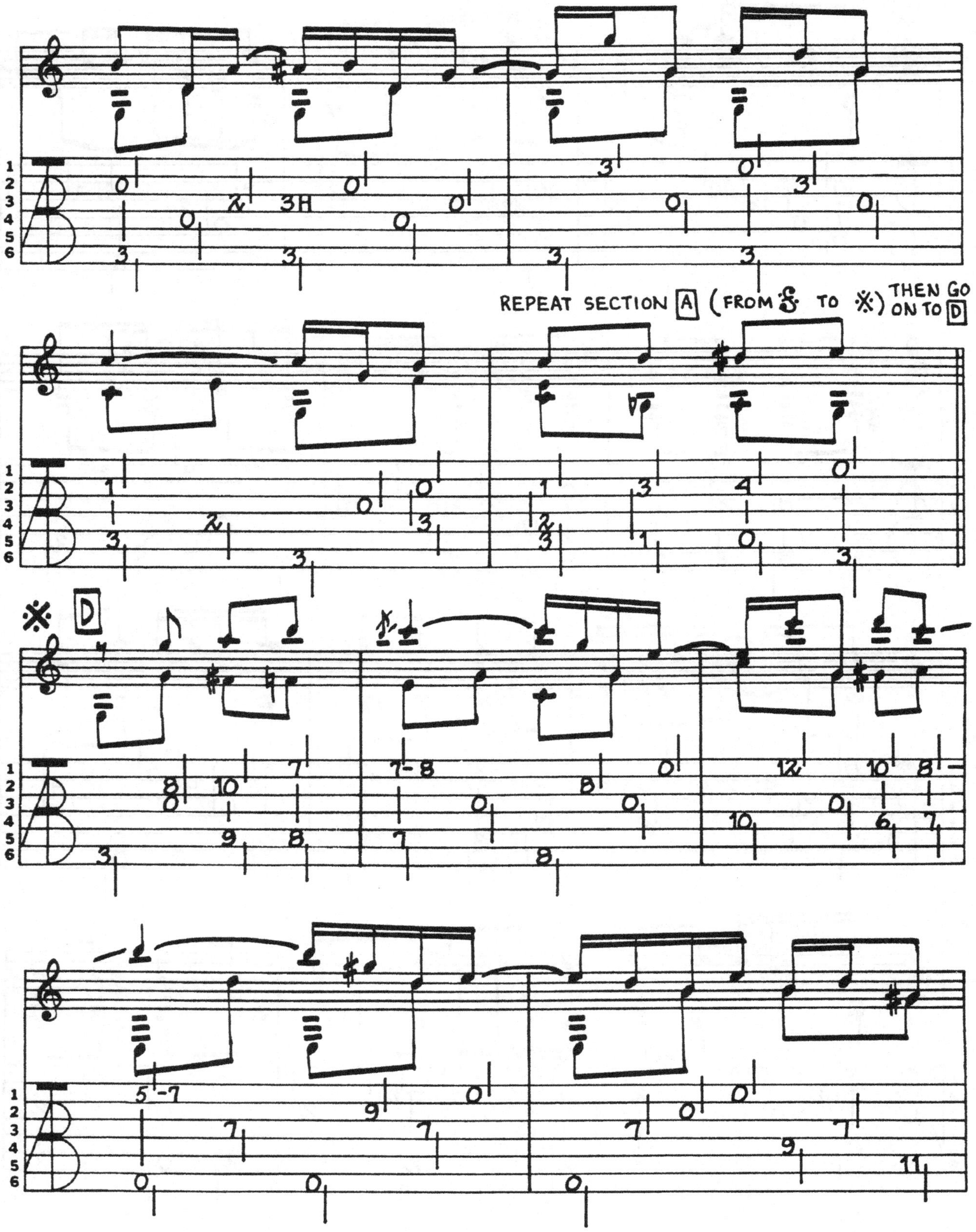
REPEAT SECTION A (FROM 𝄋 TO ※) THEN GO ON TO D
D

119

121

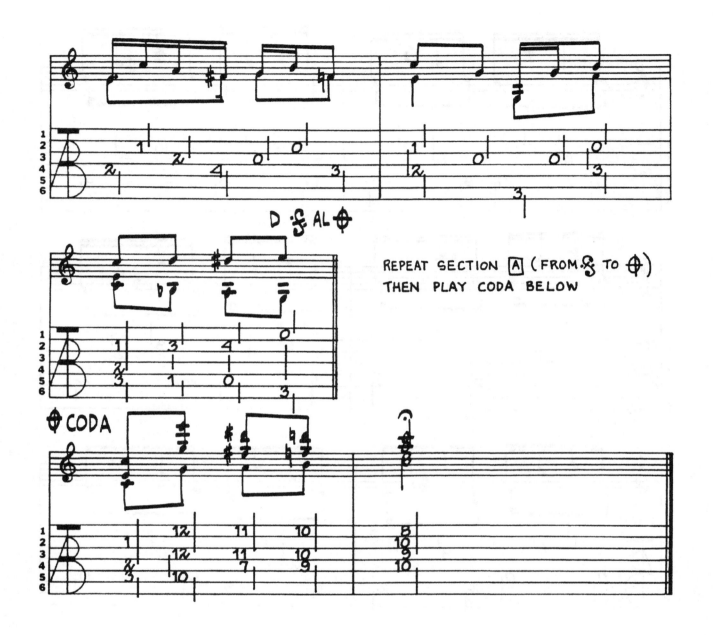

REPEAT SECTION [A] (FROM 𝄋 TO ⊕)
THEN PLAY CODA BELOW

122

BRANSLE GAY

By Gervais
Arr. John Renbourn

CAROLAN'S CONCERTO

By Turlough Carolan
Arr. John Renbourn

131

MRS. O'ROURKE

By Turlough Carolan
Arr. John Renbourn

LORD INCHIQUIN

By Turlough Carolan
Arr. John Renbourn

138

LAMENT FOR CHARLES MACCABE

By Turlough Carolan
Arr. John Renbourn

THE LAMENTATION OF OWEN ROE O'NEILL

By Turlough Carolan
Arr. John Renbourn

DISCOGRAPHY

A cassette has been prepared that features many of the arrangements presented in this collection. For information regarding this, write to Mel Bay Publications, 4 Industrial Drive, P.O. Box 66, Pacific, MO 63069, or Stefan Grossman's Guitar Workshop, P.O. Box 802, Sparta, NJ 07871.

Davey Graham, John Renbourn, and Bert Jansch have been recording fine albums for over 20 years. Many of these have been released only in Europe, and unfortunately many have long been deleted. Below is a listing of albums that I find particularly enjoyable and helpful. Some are available from Stefan Grossman's Guitar Workshop.

Davey Graham/Blues Guitar Workshop
(Guitar Workshop 127)

An anthology featuring Davey Graham, Duck Baker, Tom Paley, Sam Mitchell, and Mike Cooper. Titles by Davey Graham include: "I Just Want to Make Love to You," "Panic Room Blues," "When I've Been Drinking," and "How Come You Do Me Like You Do."

Davey Graham/The Complete Guitarist
(Guitar Workshop 131)

Titles include: "Lord Mayo," "Lord Inchiquin," "Lashtal's Room," "Ein Feste Burg," "The Road to Lisdoonvarna," "Renaissance Piece," "Hardiman the Fiddler," "Sarah," "Frieze Britches," "Blues for Gino," "The Hunter's Purse," "Prelude from the Suite in D Minor," "Fairies' Hornpipe," "40-Ton Parachute," "The Gold Ring," "Down Ampney," and "Banish Misfortune."

Davey Graham/Dance for Two People
(Kicking Mule Records)

Titles include: "Dance for Two People," "Bloody Fields of Flanders," "Indian Piece," "Lute Prelude," "She Moved Through the Bizarre," "Minuets I and II," "Reng," "Breathe on Me Breath of God," "El Cafe de Chinitas," "Happy Meeting in Glory," "Farewell to the Creeks," "Yemeni Taqsim," Mna Na Heireann," "Kim," "Lady Hunsdon's Puffe," "Wash Nha Homa," "Two Hymns," and "Uskudar."

Davey Graham/Irish Reels, Jigs, Hornpipes and Airs
(Guitar Workshop 120)

An anthology featuring Davey Graham, Duck Baker, Dave Evans, and Dan Ar Bras. Titles by Davey Graham include: "Old Hag You Have Killed Me," "The Hag with the Money," "Carrickfergus," and "The Water Is Wide."

John Renbourn/The Black Balloon
(Shanachie Records 97009)

Titles include: "The Moon Shines Bright," "The English Dance," "Bouree I and II," "The Mist Covered Mountains of Home," "The Orphan," "The Tarboulton," "The Pelican," and "The Black Balloon."

John Renbourn/The Enchanted Garden (John Renbourn Group)
(Shanachie Records 79074)

Titles include: "The Maid on the Shore," "Douce Dame Jolie," "A Bold Young Farmer," "Sidi Brahim," "Pavane 'Belle Qui Tiens Ma Vie,' " "Toudion," "The Truth from Above," "Le Tambourin," and "The Plains of Waterloo."

John Renbourn/The Hermit
(Kicking Mule Records)

Titles include: "The Hermit," "John's Tune," "Goat Island," "Old Mac Bladgitt," "Faro's Bag," "Caroline's Tune," "The Lamentation of Owen Roe O'Neill," "Lord Inchiquin," "O'Carolan's Concerto," "The Princess and the Puddings," "Pavanna (Anna Bannana)," "A Toye," and "Lord Willoughby's Welcome Home."

John Renbourn/In Concert (with Stefan Grossman)
(Shanachie Records 95001)

Titles include: "Looper's Corner," "The Shoes of the Fisherman's Wife Are Some Jive Ass Slippers," "Twelve Sticks," "Cocaine Blues," "Tightrope," "Medley: Sheebeg An Sheemore/Drunken Wagoner," "Medley: Cincinnati Flow Bag/New York City Bag/Hot Dogs," "Medley: Judy/Angie," "Medley: Lament for Owen Roe O'Neill/Mist Covered Mountains of Home," "Great Dreams from Heaven," "Sweet Potato," "Goodbye Porkpie Hat," "Midnight on the Water," "Spirit Levels," and "Mississippi Blues No. 2."

John Renbourn/A Maid in Bedlam (John Renbourn Group)
(Shanachie Records 79004)

Titles include: "Black Waterside," "Nacht Tanz/Shaeffertanz," "A Maid in Bedlam," "Gypsy Dance/Jews Dance," "John Barleycorn," "Renardine," "My Johnny Was a Shoemaker," "Death and the Lady," "The Battle of Augrham/5 in a Line," and "Talk About Suffering."

John Renbourn/Snap a Little Owl (with Stefan Grossman)
(Shanachie Records 97004)

Titles include: "Spirit Levels," "Water Gypsy," "Snap a Little Owl," "Bermuda Triangle Exit," "Looper's Corner," "Luke's Little Summer," "Woman from Donori," "Why a Duck," "Idaho Potato," "Luckett Sunday," "All Things Parallel Must Converge," "The Way She Walks," and "The Drifter."

John Renbourn/The Three Kingdoms (with Stefan Grossman)
(Shanachie Records 95006)

Titles include: "The Three Kingdoms," "Round About Midnight," "Dollar Town," "Catwalk," "Cherry," "Rites of Passage," "Medley: Kiera's Dream/Parson's Mud," "Keeper of the Vine," "Minuet in D Minor," "Farewell to Mr. Mingus," and "Medley: Abide with Me/Old Gloryland."

Bert Jansch/Avocet (with Martin Jenkins)
(Kicking Mule Records)

Titles include: "Avocet," "Lapwing," "Kingfisher," "Kittiwake," "Bittern," and "Osprey."

Bert Jansch/The Best of Bert Jansch
(Kicking Mule Records)
Titles include: "Nicola," "Reynardine," "So Long," "Alman," "Peregrinations," "Weeping Willow Blues," "Angie," "The First Time Ever I Saw Your Face," "Nottamun Town," "It Don't Bother Me," "Box of Love," "Henry Martin," and "Needle of Death."

Bert Jansch/A Rare Conundrum
(Kicking Mule Records)
Titles include: "Daybreak," "One to a Hundred," "Pretty Saro," "Doctor Doctor," "3 A.M.," "The Curragh of Kildare," "Instrumentally Irish," "St. Fiacre," "If You See My Love," "Looking for a Home," "Poor Mouth," "Cat and Mouse," "Three Chord Trick," and "Lost Love."

Bert Jansch/Thirteen Down
(Guitar Workshop 130)
Titles include: "Bridge," "Sovay," "Let Me Sing About Love," "Time and Time," "A Single Rose," "In My Mind," "Down River," "Una Line a di Dolcezza," "Where'd My Life Go," "If I Had a Lover," "Nightfall," "Sweet Mother Earth," and "Ask Your Daddy."

John Renbourn has prepared a series of taped guitar lessons that are available from Stefan Grossman's Guitar Workshop. He teaches the following tunes on these cassettes: "Judy," "Buffalo," "Bransle Gay," "The English Dance," "Lady Nothynge's Toye Puffe," "My Dear Boy," "Transfusion," "Sweet Potato," "Mist Covered Mountains of Home," and "The Orphan."

Bert Jansch has a book available in England from New Punchbowl Music, Leigh Heights, Haslemere Road, Hind Head, Surrey, England. This includes 14 of Bert's songs and instrumentals.

From Chappell Publications in France, there is available a book of tablature of Bert Jansch/John Renbourn arrangements. For information regarding this, write Chappell SA., 12 Rue De Penthievre, 75008 Paris, France.

A collection titled *Art of Fingerstyle Guitar/Guitar Duets* by Stefan Grossman and John Renbourn is available from Mel Bay Publications, P.O. Box 66, Pacific, MO 63069.

For information regarding the British folk scene, I strongly recommend a subscription to *Folk Roots*, P.O. Box 337, London N4 1T2, England. This excellent magazine has interviews, club listings, record reviews, and general all-around information about the goings-on in the British folk clubs.

NOTES

NOTES

NOTES

Made in the USA
Coppell, TX
26 June 2024

33966044R00090